Pebble® Plus

Physical Science

Magnetism

by Abbie Dunne

CAPSTONE PRESS
a capstone imprint

Pebble Plus is published by Capstone Press,
1710 Roe Crest Drive, North Mankato, Minnesota 56003
www.mycapstone.com

Library of Congress Cataloging-in-Publication Data
Names: Dunne, Abbie, author.
Title: Magnetism / by Abbie Dunne.
Description: North Mankato, Minnesota : Capstone Press, [2017] | Series:
  Pebble plus. Physical science | Audience: Ages 4-8. | Audience: K to
  grade 3. | Includes bibliographical references and index.
Identifiers: LCCN 2016005331| ISBN 9781515709381 (library binding) | ISBN
  9781515709701 (pbk.) | ISBN 9781515711056 (ebook (pdf)
Subjects: LCSH: Magnetism—Juvenile literature. | Magnets—Juvenile
  literature.
Classification: LCC QC757.5 .D86 2017 | DDC 538—dc23
LC record available at http://lccn.loc.gov/2016005331

Editorial Credits

Linda Staniford, editor; Veronica Scott, designer; Eric Gohl, media researcher;
Katy LaVigne, production specialist

Photo Credits

Capstone Studio: Karon Dubke, cover, 5, 17, 20; Shutterstock: bikeriderlondon, 9, Hung Chung
Chih, 15, imagedb.com. 11, Lena Lir, 7, Snowbelle, 13, wavebreakmedia, 19

Design Elements: Shutterstock

Note to Parents and Teachers

The Physical Science set supports national curriculum standards for science. This book introduces
the concept of magnetism. The images support early readers in understanding the text. The
repetition of words and phrases helps early readers in understanding the text. This book also
introduces early readers to subject-specific vocabulary words, which are defined in the Glossary
section. Early readers may need assistance to read some words and to use the Table of Contents,
Glossary, Read More, Internet Sites, Critical Thinking Using the Common Core, and Index sections
of the book.

Printed and bound in China.
007701

Table of Contents

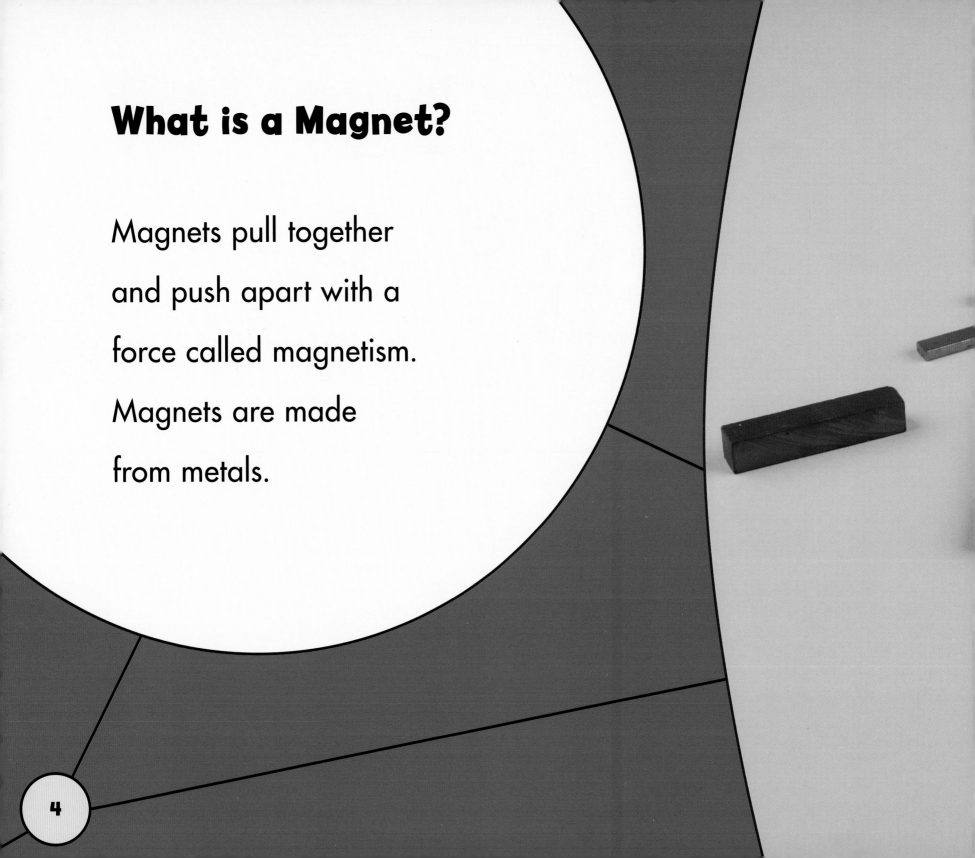

What is a Magnet?

Magnets pull together
and push apart with a
force called magnetism.
Magnets are made
from metals.

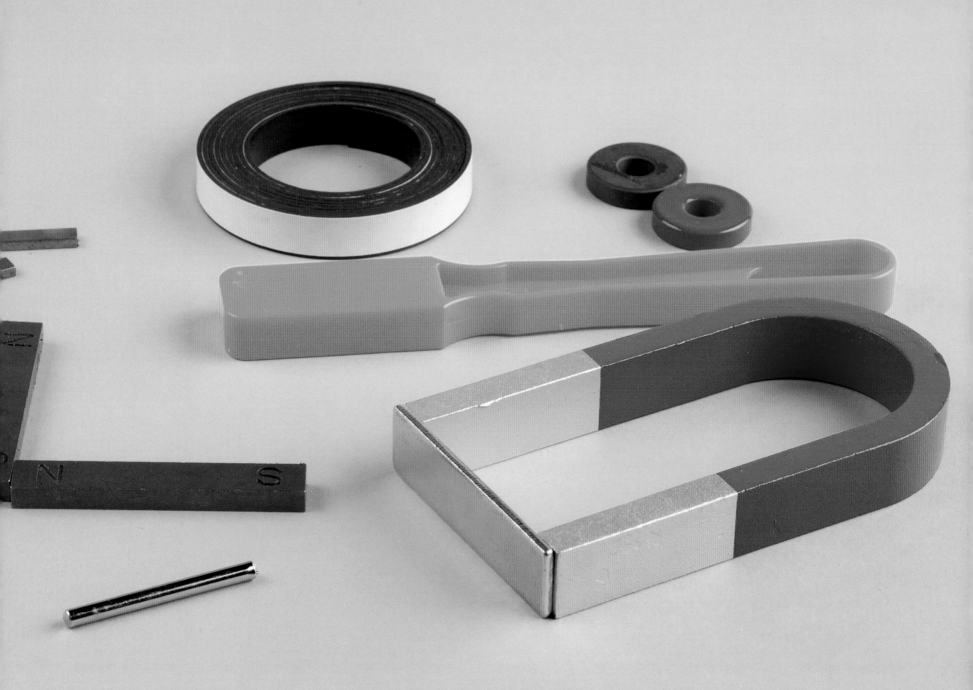

Magnetic Materials

All magnets attract objects made of iron. Nails and paper clips stick to magnets. Other metals do not stick to magnets.

Magnetic Field

Like a bubble, a magnetic
field surrounds a magnet.
If the magnet is close to
a magnetic object, its magnetic
field pulls the object toward it.

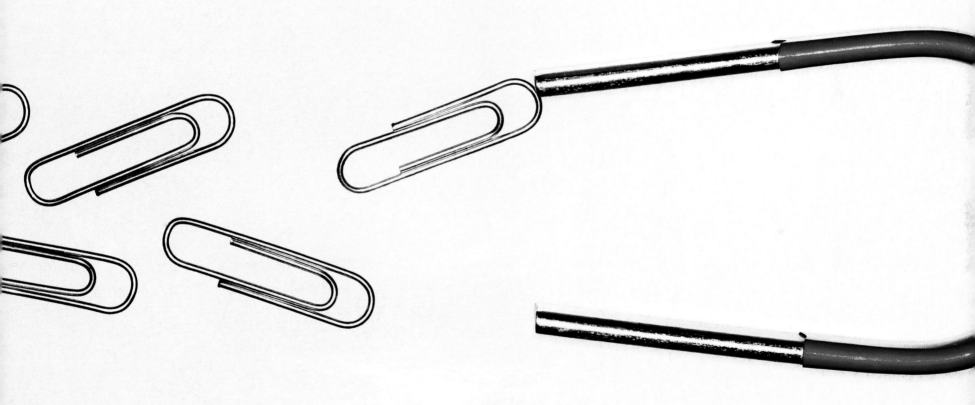

9

A magnet's ends are called poles. Every magnet has a north and south pole. Opposite poles attract each other. Poles that are the same repel each other.

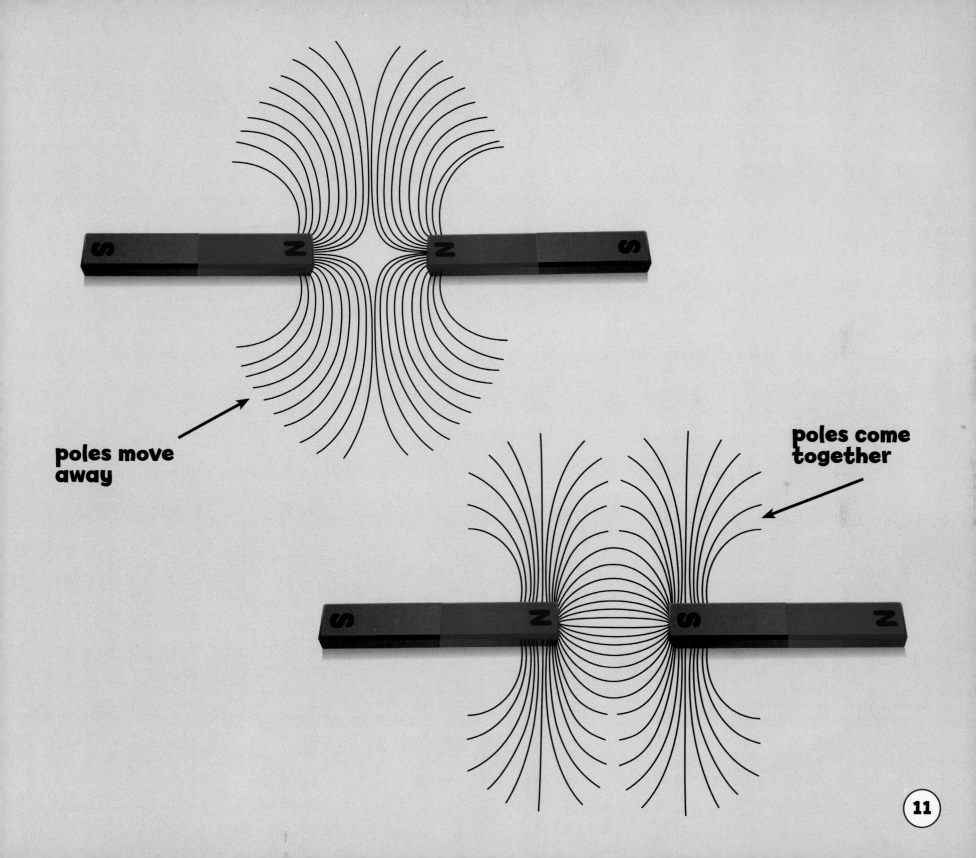

poles move
away

poles come
together

11

Earth has an iron core. Just like a magnet, Earth has a magnetic field. Earth also has a North Pole and a South Pole.

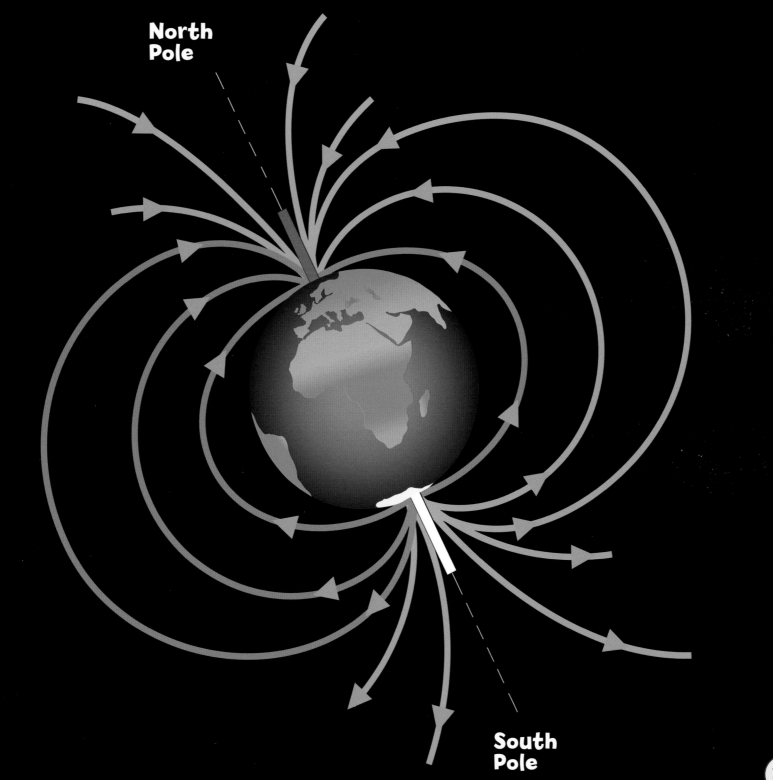

North
Pole

magnetic
field

South
Pole

13

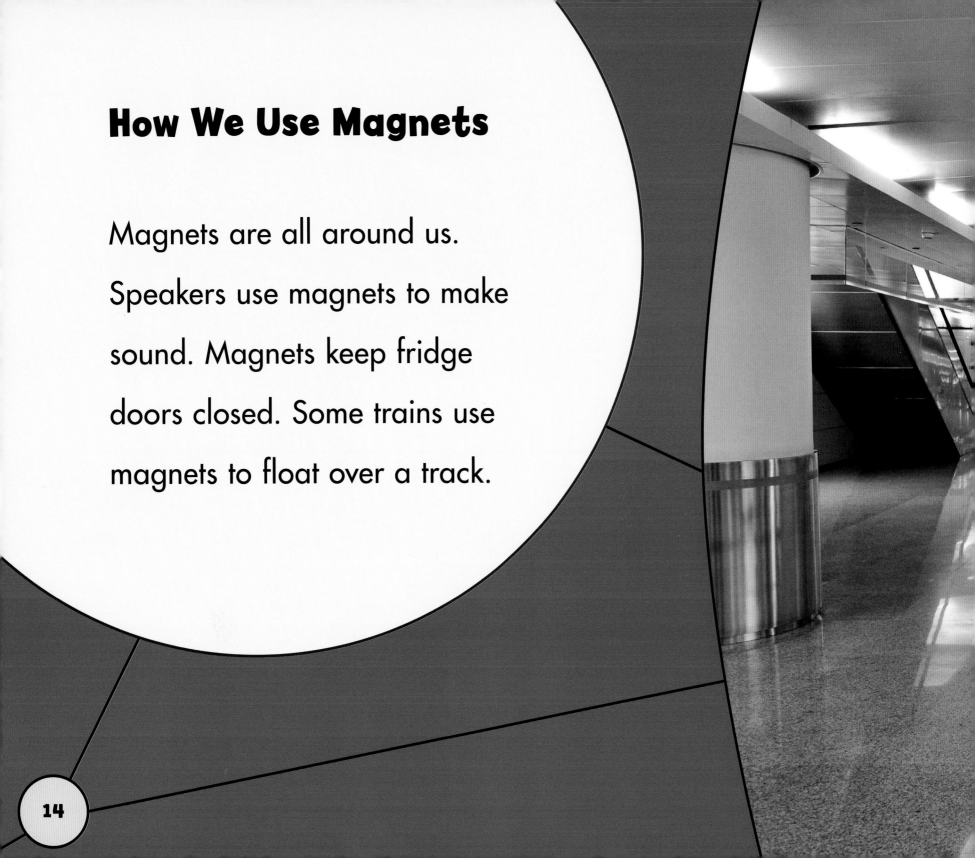

How We Use Magnets

Magnets are all around us. Speakers use magnets to make sound. Magnets keep fridge doors closed. Some trains use magnets to float over a track.

15

A magnetic field can pass through materials such as paper, water, and glass. A magnet can hold a piece of paper on to a metal fridge door.

A compass has a magnet
in the shape of a needle.
The needle moves in a circle
until it points to north.
This helps people find their way.

Activity

How far apart can two magnets be and still attract or repel each other? Write down how far apart you think they can be. Then find out!

What You Need

- 2 bar magnets with north and south poles marked

- 3-inch x 5-inch (7.6-cm x 12.7-cm) index cards

- ruler

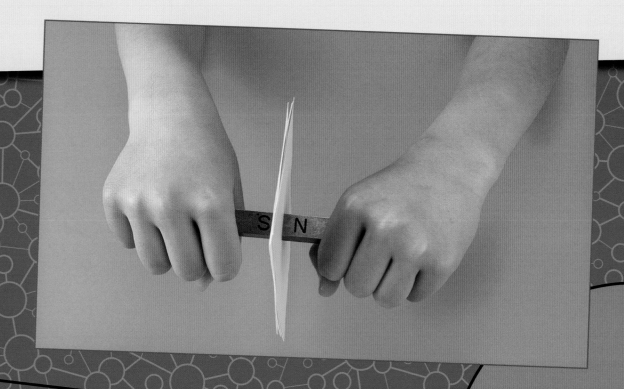

What You Do

1. Place the magnets so they pull on each other and touch.

2. Put five index cards between the magnets. Wiggle the cards to show that the magnets are pulling on each other.

3. Put five more index cards between the magnets. Wiggle the cards to show that the magnets are pulling on each other.

4. Keep adding index cards, five at a time, until the magnets stop pulling on each other. Count how many cards there are between the magnets.

5. Use the ruler to measure how far apart the magnets are when they stop pulling each other.

What Do You Think?

Make a claim about magnets. A claim is something you believe to be true. Do magnets need to touch each other to push and pull each other?

Use facts from your test.

Glossary

attract—to pull something toward something else

compass—an instrument used for finding directions

force—push or pull

magnetic field—the space around a magnetic object in which magnetic forces can be detected

pole—one of the two ends of a magnet; a pole can also be the top or bottom part of a planet

repel—to push something away

Read More

Rising, Trudy L. *Is It Magnetic or Nonmagnetic? What's the Matter?* New York: Crabtree Pub. Company, 2012.

Royston, Angela. *All About Magnetism.* Chicago: Heinemann Raintree, 2016.

Swanson, Jennifer. *The Attractive Truth About Magnetism.* North Mankato, Minn.: Capstone Press, 2013.

Internet Sites

FactHound offers a safe, fun way to find Internet sites related to this book. All of the sites on FactHound have been researched by our staff.

Here's all you do:

Visit *www.facthound.com*

Type in this code: 9781515709381

 Check out projects, games and lots more at **www.capstonekids.com**

Critical Thinking Using the Common Core

1. If you hold the north poles of two magnets near each other, will they pull together (attract) or push apart (repel)?
(Key Ideas and Details)

2. Magnets are everywhere. Can you think of a magnet you use often? (Integration of Knowledge and Ideas)

3. Could you use a magnet to pick up an aluminum can? Why or why not?
(Integration of Knowledge and Ideas)

Index